GRAPHIC LIBRARY™

GRAPHIC HISTORY

NAT TURNER'S SLAVE REBELLION

by Michael Burgan

Illustrated by Richard Dominguez,
Bob Wiacek, and Charles Barnett III

Consultant:
Theodore C. DeLaney, PhD
Associate Professor of History
Washington and Lee University
Lexington, Virginia

Capstone
press

Mankato, Minnesota

Graphic Library is published by Capstone Press,
1710 Roe Crest Drive, North Mankato, Minnesota 56003.
www.capstonepub.com

Library of Congress Cataloging-in-Publication Data
Burgan, Michael.
Nat Turner's slave rebellion / by Michael Burgan; illustrated by Richard Dominguez, Bob Wiacek, and Charles Barnett III.
p. cm.—(Graphic library. Graphic history)
Includes bibliographical references and index.
ISBN: 978-0-7368-5490-0 (hardcover)
ISBN: 978-0-7368-6879-2 (softcover pbk.)
1. Turner, Nat, 1800?–1831—Juvenile literature. 2. Southampton Insurrection, 1831—Juvenile literature. 3. Slaves—Virginia—Southampton County—Biography—Juvenile literature. 4. Slave insurrections—Virginia—Southampton County—History—19th century—Juvenile literature. 5. Southampton County (Va.)—History—19th century—Juvenile literature. I. Dominguez, Richard, ill. II. Wiacek, Bob, ill. III. Barnett, Charles, III, ill. IV. Title. V. Series.
F232.S7B87 2006
975.5'5503092—dc22 2005029332

Summary: In graphic novel format, tells the true story of the 1831 Virginia slave rebellion led by slave Nat Turner, who believed he was a prophet.

Art Direction
Bob Lentz

Designer
Thomas Emery

Storyboard Artist
Blake A. Hoena

Production Designer
Kim Brown

Colorist
Sarah Trover

Editor
Christine Peterson

Editor's note: Direct quotations from primary sources are indicated by a yellow background.

Direct quotations appear on the following pages:
Page 21, from a September 1831 article by John Pleasants printed in *The Constitutional Whig*, Richmond, Virginia; page 22, from the Court Records of Southampton County, Virginia, August 31, 1831; page 23, from an article in *The Petersburg Intelligencer*, Petersburg, Virginia, originally printed in November 1831, as published in *The Southampton Slave Revolt of 1831*, by Henry Irving Tragle (New York: Vintage Books, 1973).

Printed in the United States 5961

TABLE OF CONTENTS

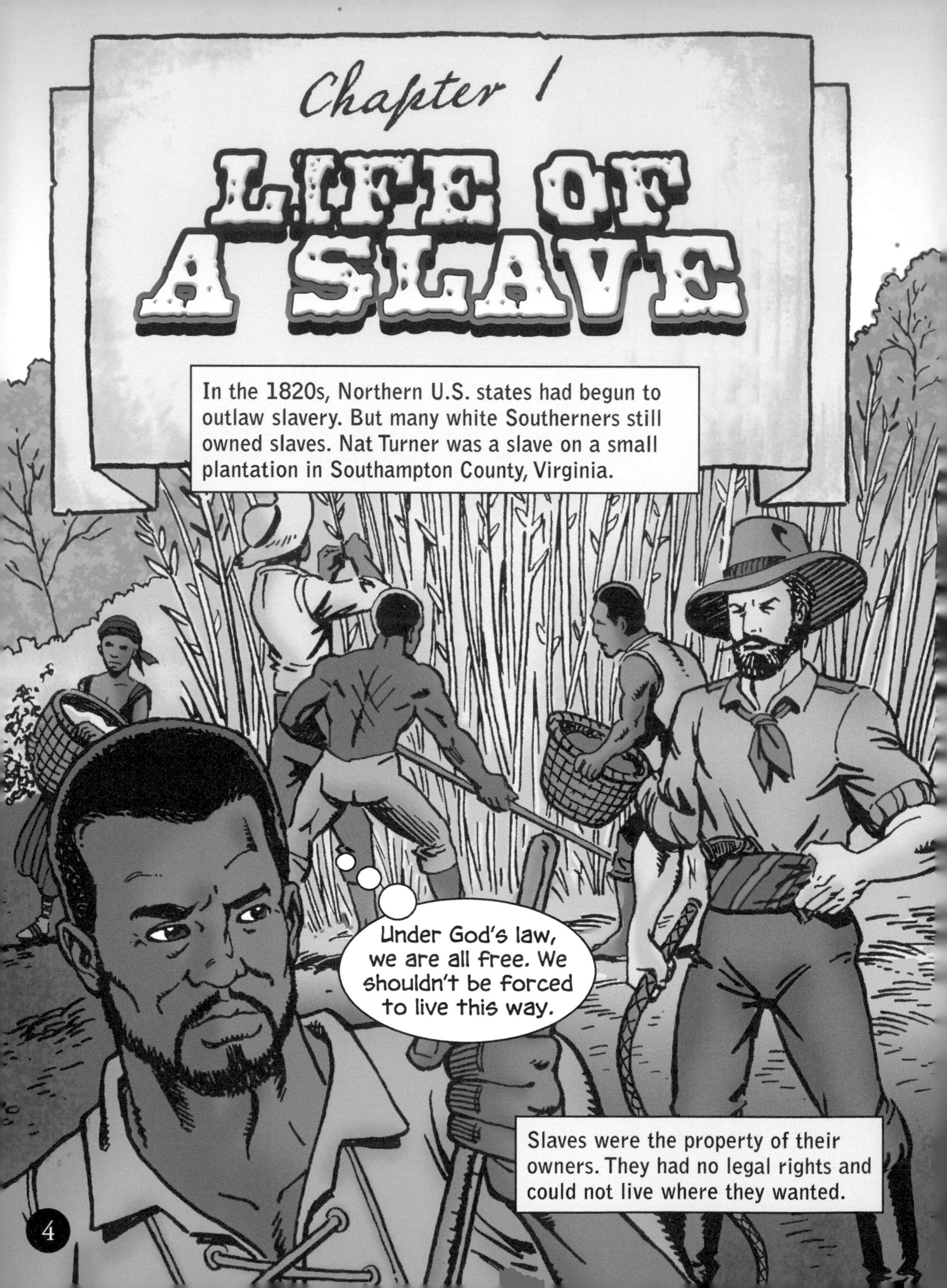
Chapter 1
LIFE OF A SLAVE
In the 1820s, Northern U.S. states had begun to outlaw slavery. But many white Southerners still owned slaves. Nat Turner was a slave on a small plantation in Southampton County, Virginia.
Under God's law, we are all free. We shouldn't be forced to live this way.
Slaves were the property of their owners. They had no legal rights and could not live where they wanted.

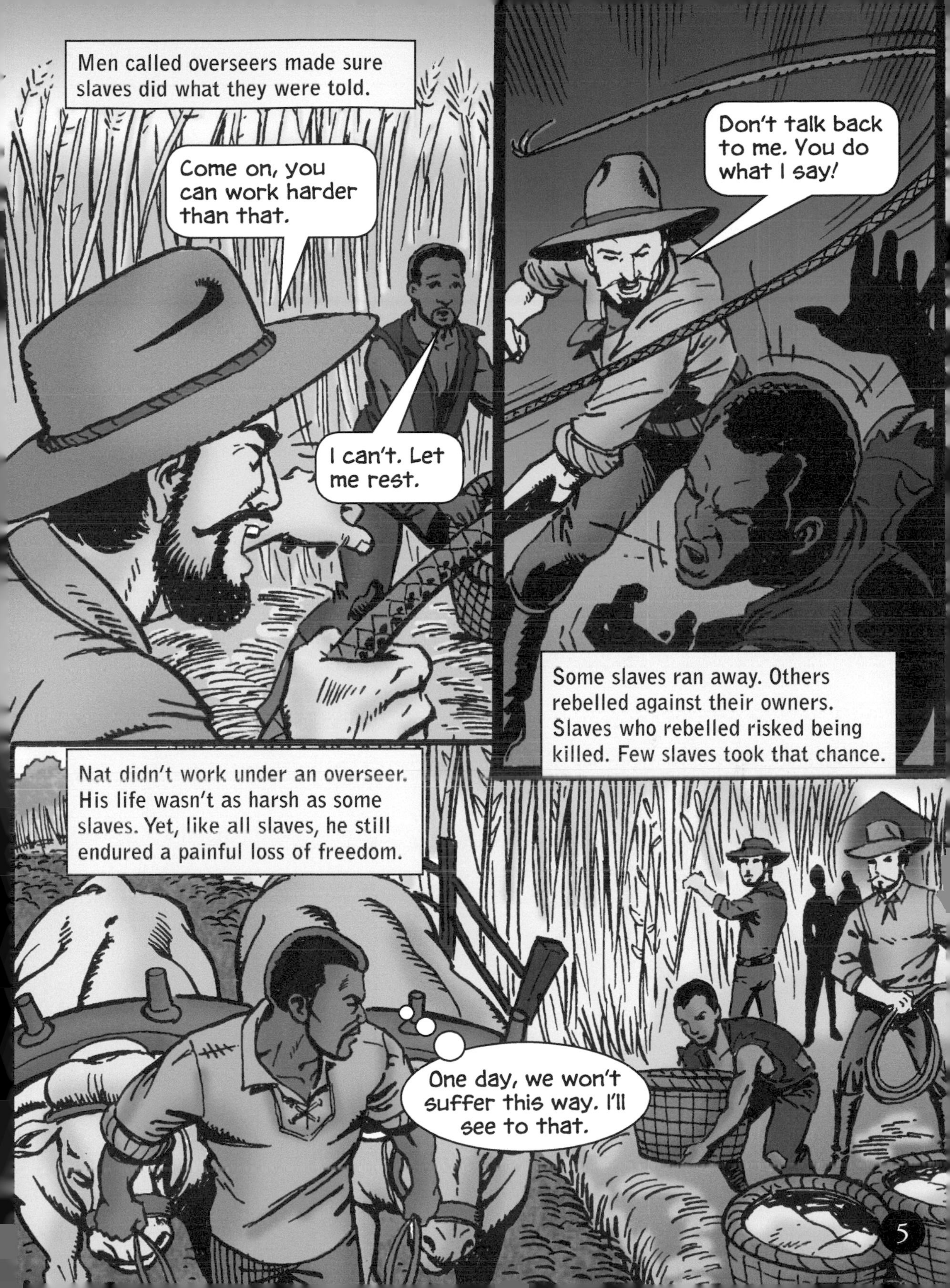
Men called overseers made sure slaves did what they were told.
Come on, you can work harder than that.
I can't. Let me rest.
Don't talk back to me. You do what I say!
Some slaves ran away. Others rebelled against their owners. Slaves who rebelled risked being killed. Few slaves took that chance.
Nat didn't work under an overseer. His life wasn't as harsh as some slaves. Yet, like all slaves, he still endured a painful loss of freedom.
One day, we won't suffer this way. I'll see to that.

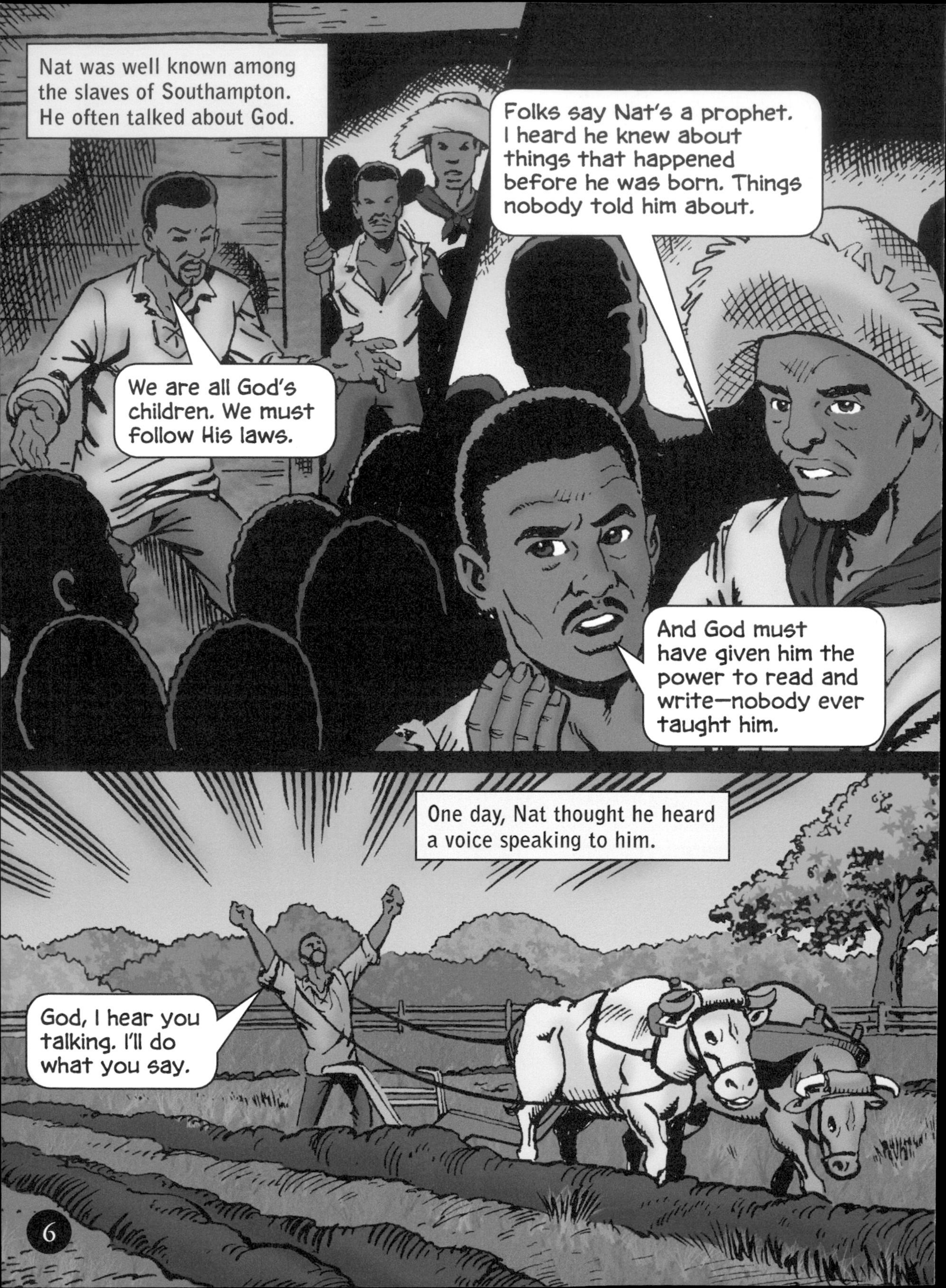
Nat was well known among the slaves of Southampton. He often talked about God.
We are all God's children. We must follow His laws.
Folks say Nat's a prophet. I heard he knew about things that happened before he was born. Things nobody told him about.
And God must have given him the power to read and write—nobody ever taught him.
One day, Nat thought he heard a voice speaking to him.
God, I hear you talking. I'll do what you say.

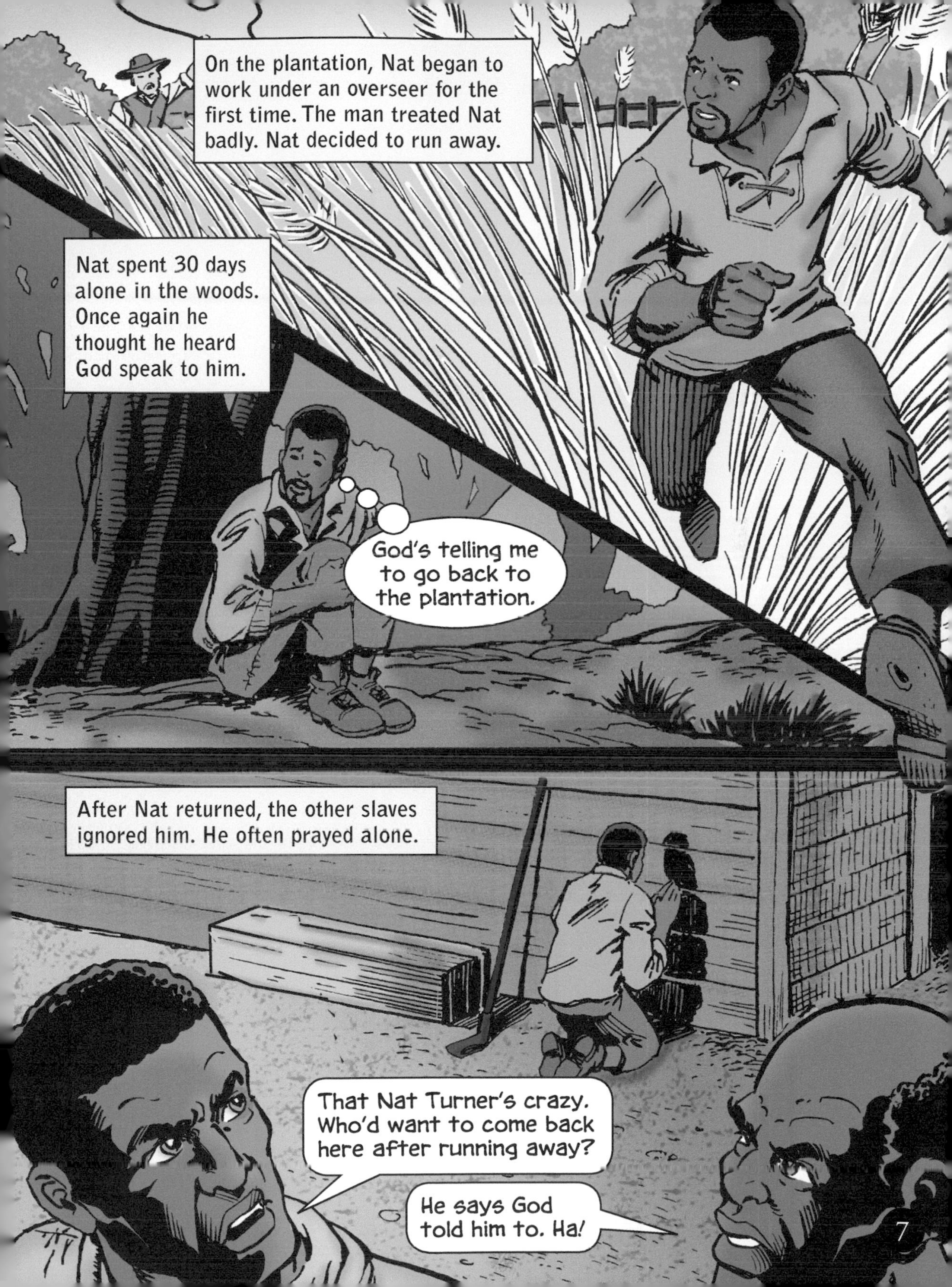

On the plantation, Nat began to work under an overseer for the first time. The man treated Nat badly. Nat decided to run away.
Nat spent 30 days alone in the woods. Once again he thought he heard God speak to him.
God's telling me to go back to the plantation.
After Nat returned, the other slaves ignored him. He often prayed alone.
That Nat Turner's crazy. Who'd want to come back here after running away?
He says God told him to. Ha!

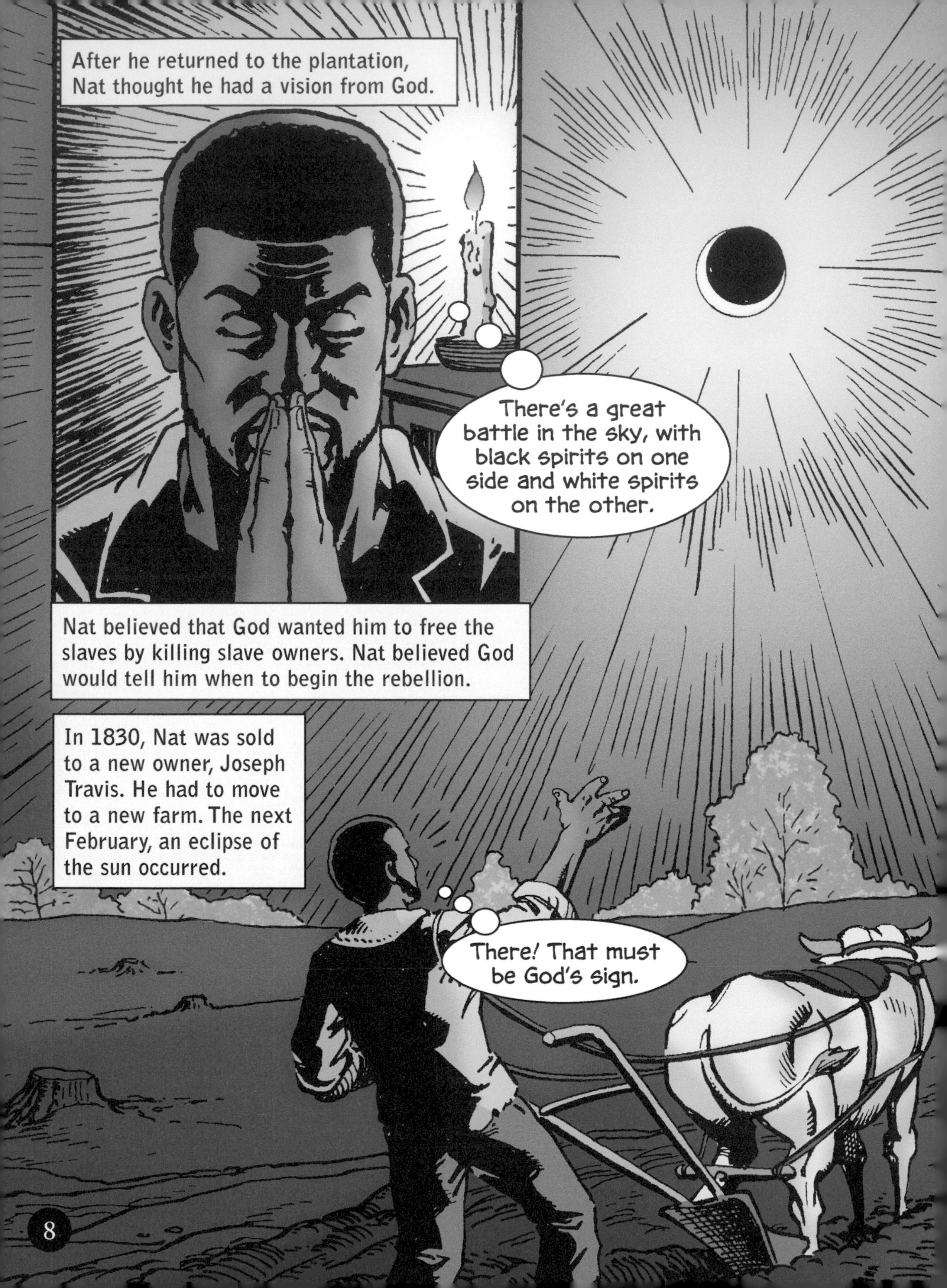
After he returned to the plantation, Nat thought he had a vision from God.
There's a great battle in the sky, with black spirits on one side and white spirits on the other.
Nat believed that God wanted him to free the slaves by killing slave owners. Nat believed God would tell him when to begin the rebellion.
In 1830, Nat was sold to a new owner, Joseph Travis. He had to move to a new farm. The next February, an eclipse of the sun occurred.
There! That must be God's sign.

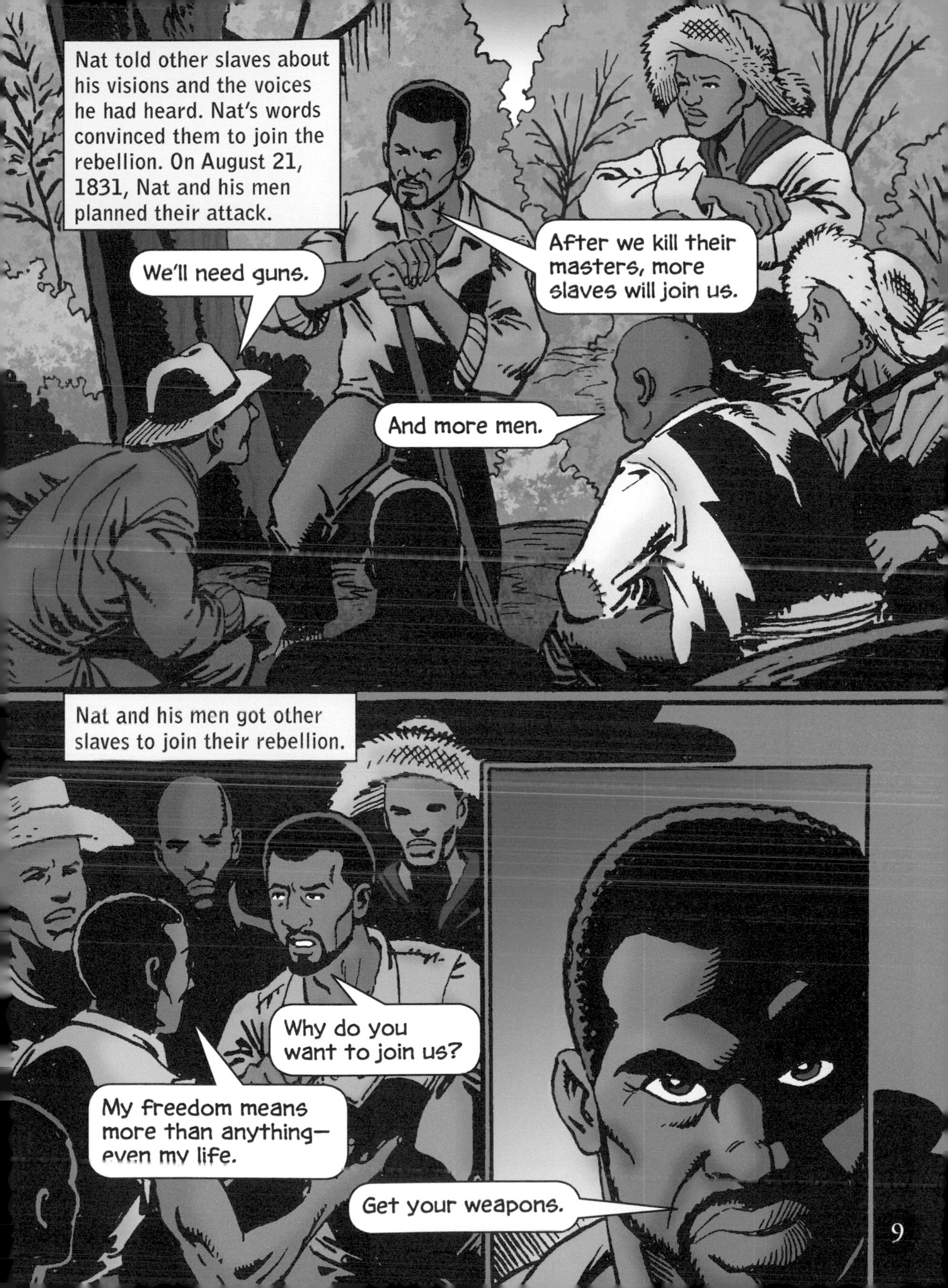
Nat told other slaves about his visions and the voices he had heard. Nat's words convinced them to join the rebellion. On August 21, 1831, Nat and his men planned their attack.
We'll need guns.
After we kill their masters, more slaves will join us.
And more men.
Nat and his men got other slaves to join their rebellion.
Why do you want to join us?
My freedom means more than anything— even my life.
Get your weapons.

Chapter 2
THE REBELLION BEGINS

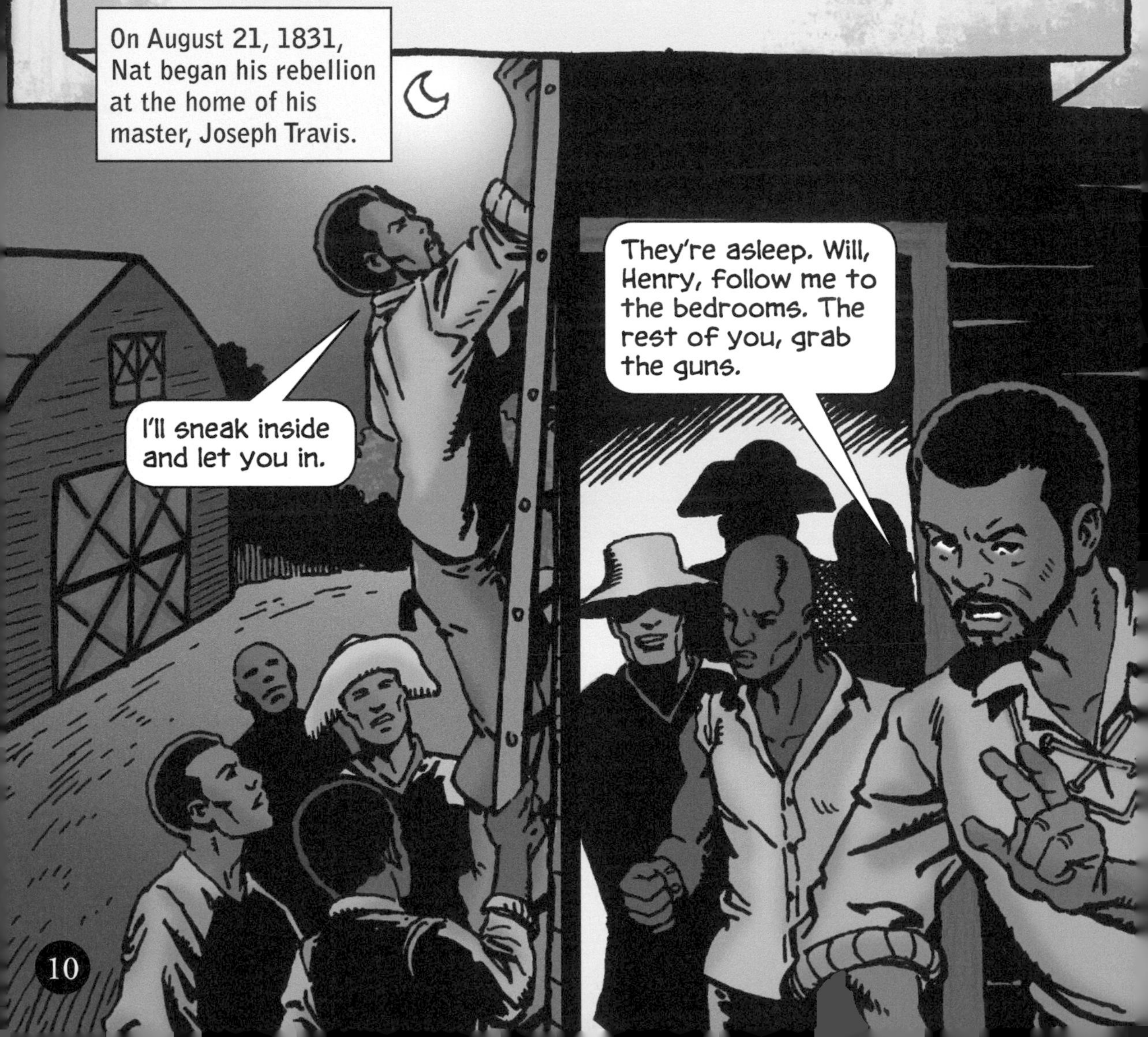

On August 21, 1831, Nat began his rebellion at the home of his master, Joseph Travis.
I'll sneak inside and let you in.
They're asleep. Will, Henry, follow me to the bedrooms. The rest of you, grab the guns.

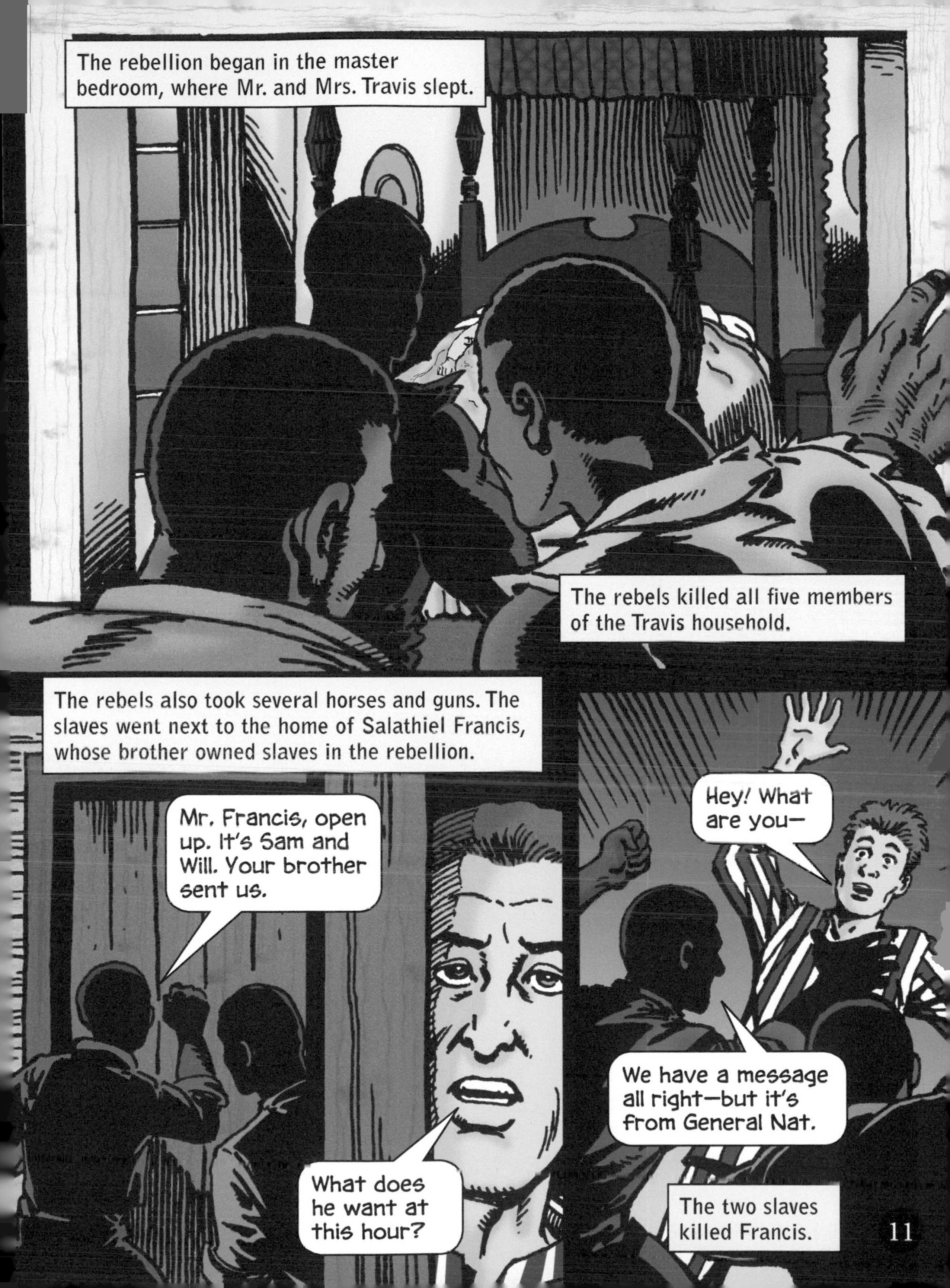
The rebellion began in the master bedroom, where Mr. and Mrs. Travis slept.
The rebels killed all five members of the Travis household.
The rebels also took several horses and guns. The slaves went next to the home of Salathiel Francis, whose brother owned slaves in the rebellion.
Mr. Francis, open up. It's Sam and Will. Your brother sent us.
What does he want at this hour?
Hey! What are you—
We have a message all right—but it's from General Nat.
The two slaves killed Francis.

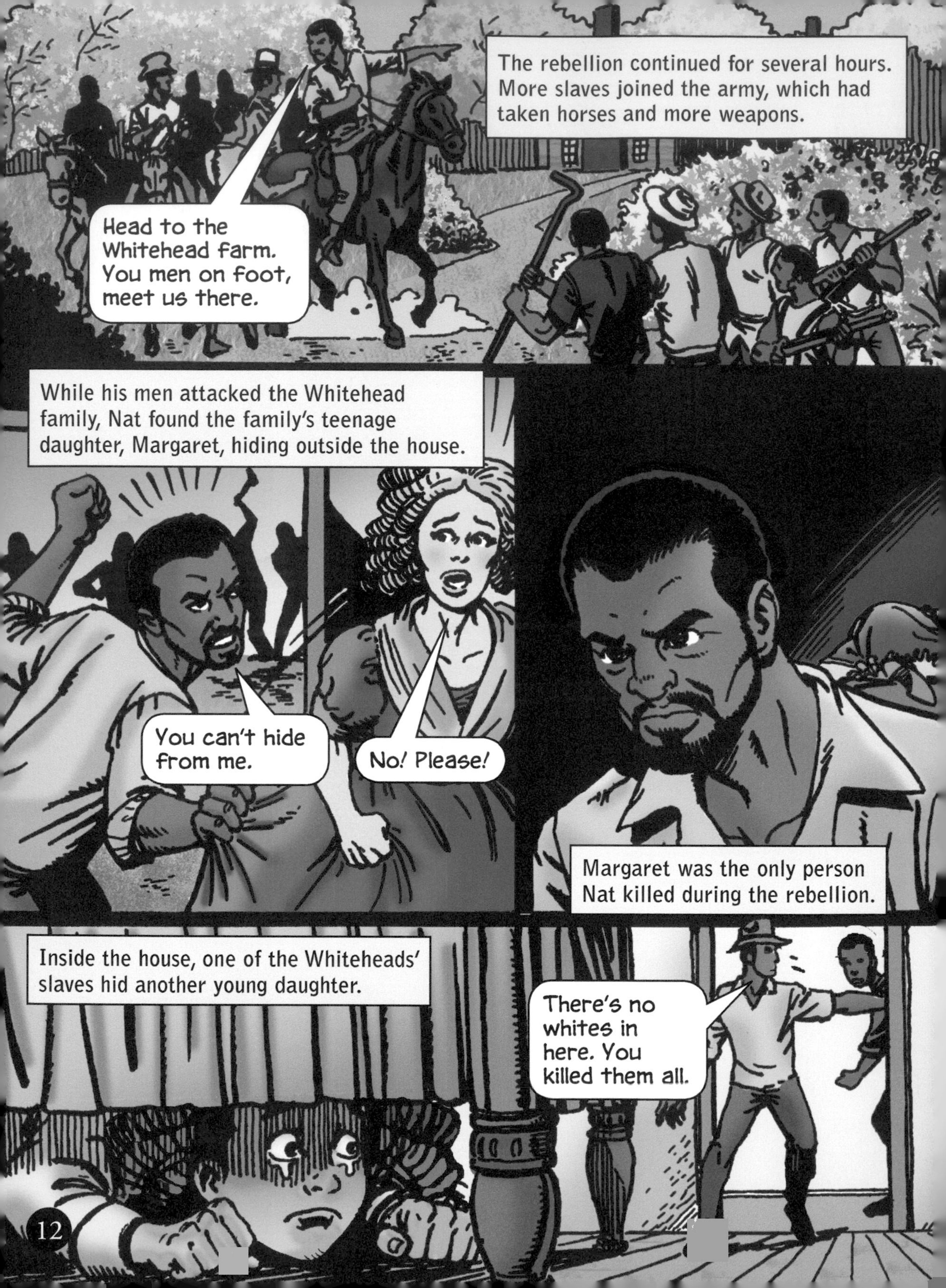
The rebellion continued for several hours. More slaves joined the army, which had taken horses and more weapons.
Head to the Whitehead farm. You men on foot, meet us there.
While his men attacked the Whitehead family, Nat found the family's teenage daughter, Margaret, hiding outside the house.
You can't hide from me.
No! Please!
Margaret was the only person Nat killed during the rebellion.
Inside the house, one of the Whiteheads' slaves hid another young daughter.
There's no whites in here. You killed them all.

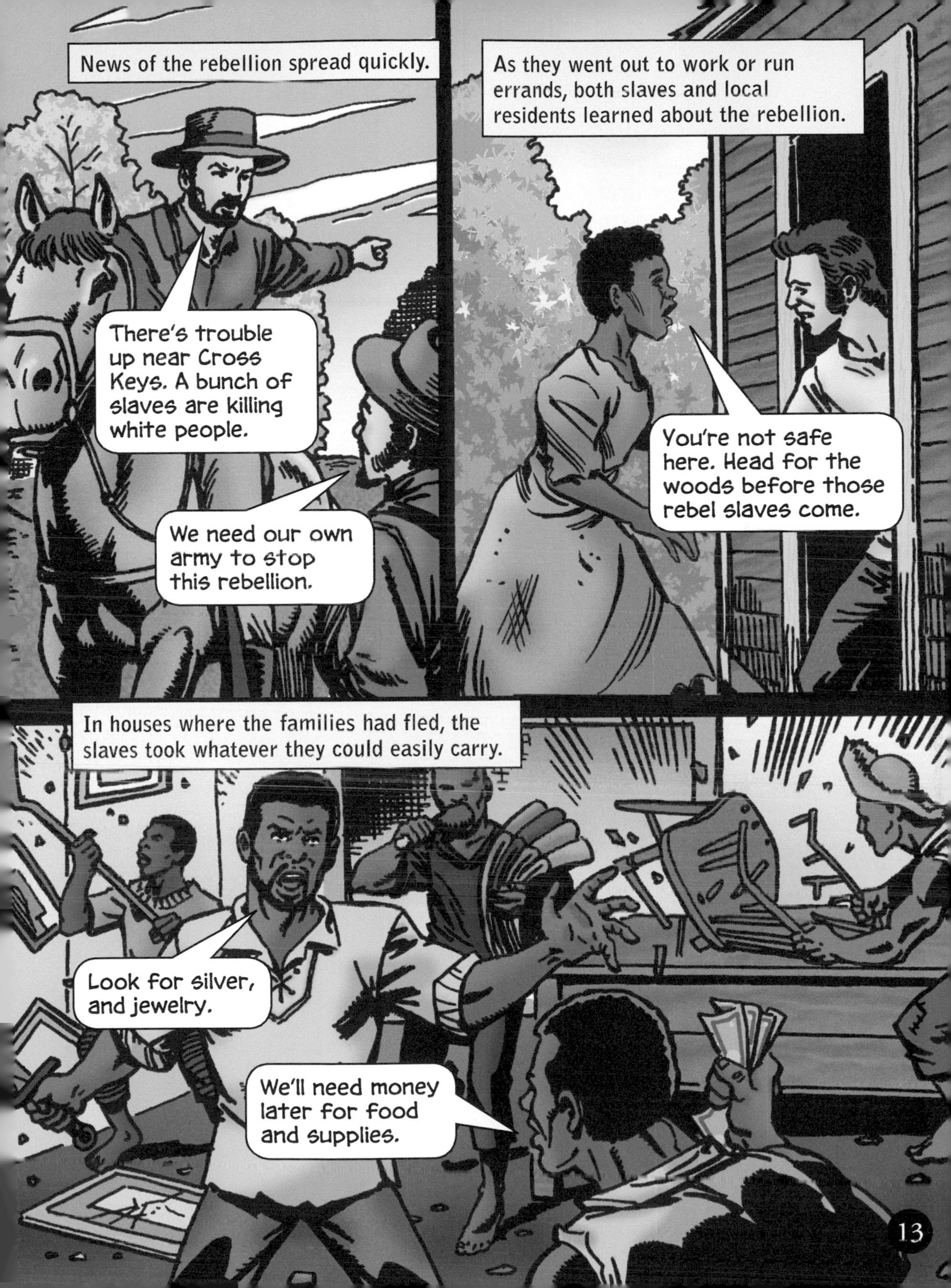
News of the rebellion spread quickly.
There's trouble up near Cross Keys. A bunch of slaves are killing white people.
We need our own army to stop this rebellion.
As they went out to work or run errands, both slaves and local residents learned about the rebellion.
You're not safe here. Head for the woods before those rebel slaves come.
In houses where the families had fled, the slaves took whatever they could easily carry.
Look for silver, and jewelry.
We'll need money later for food and supplies.

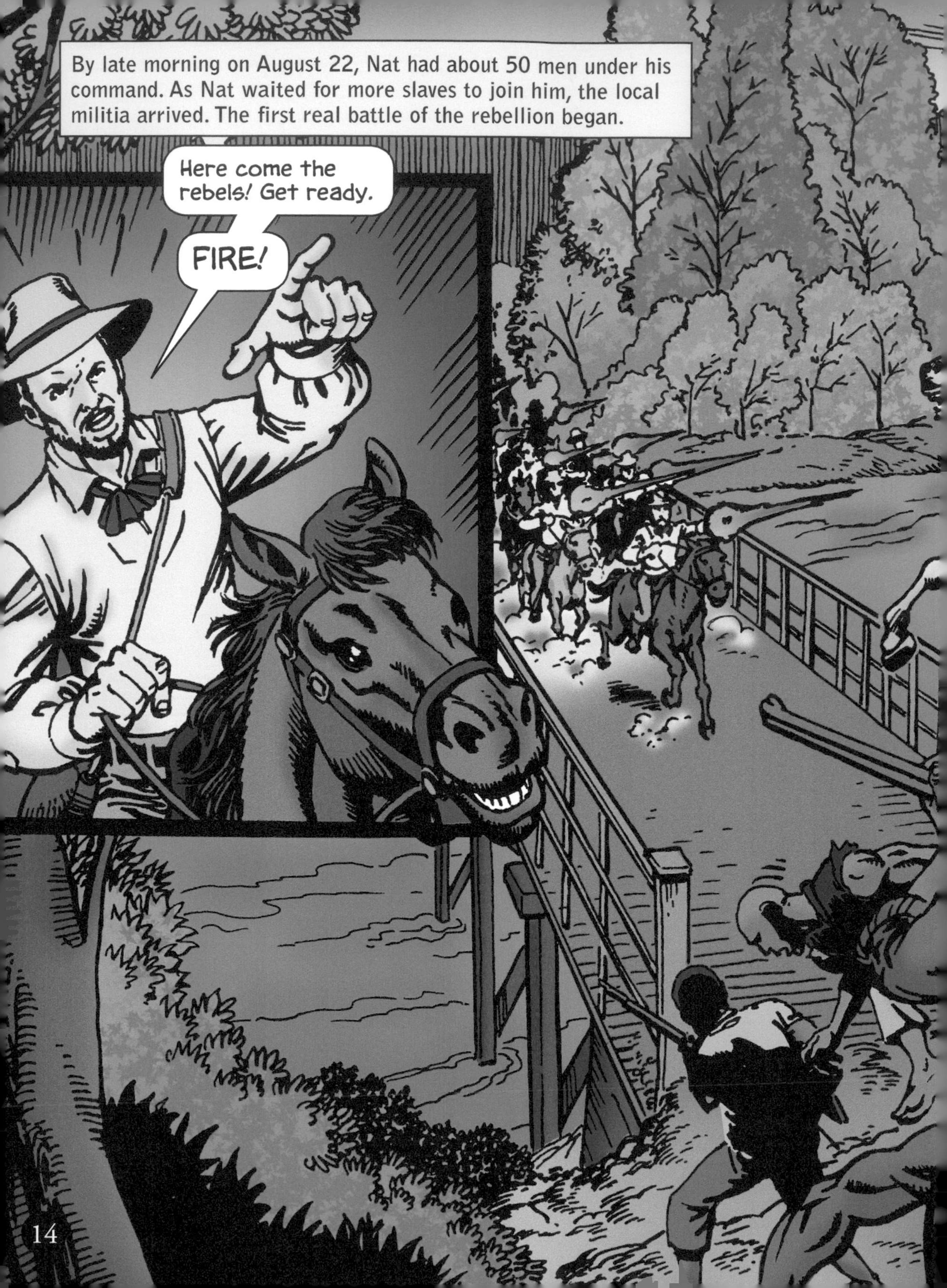
By late morning on August 22, Nat had about 50 men under his command. As Nat waited for more slaves to join him, the local militia arrived. The first real battle of the rebellion began.
Here come the rebels! Get ready.
FIRE!

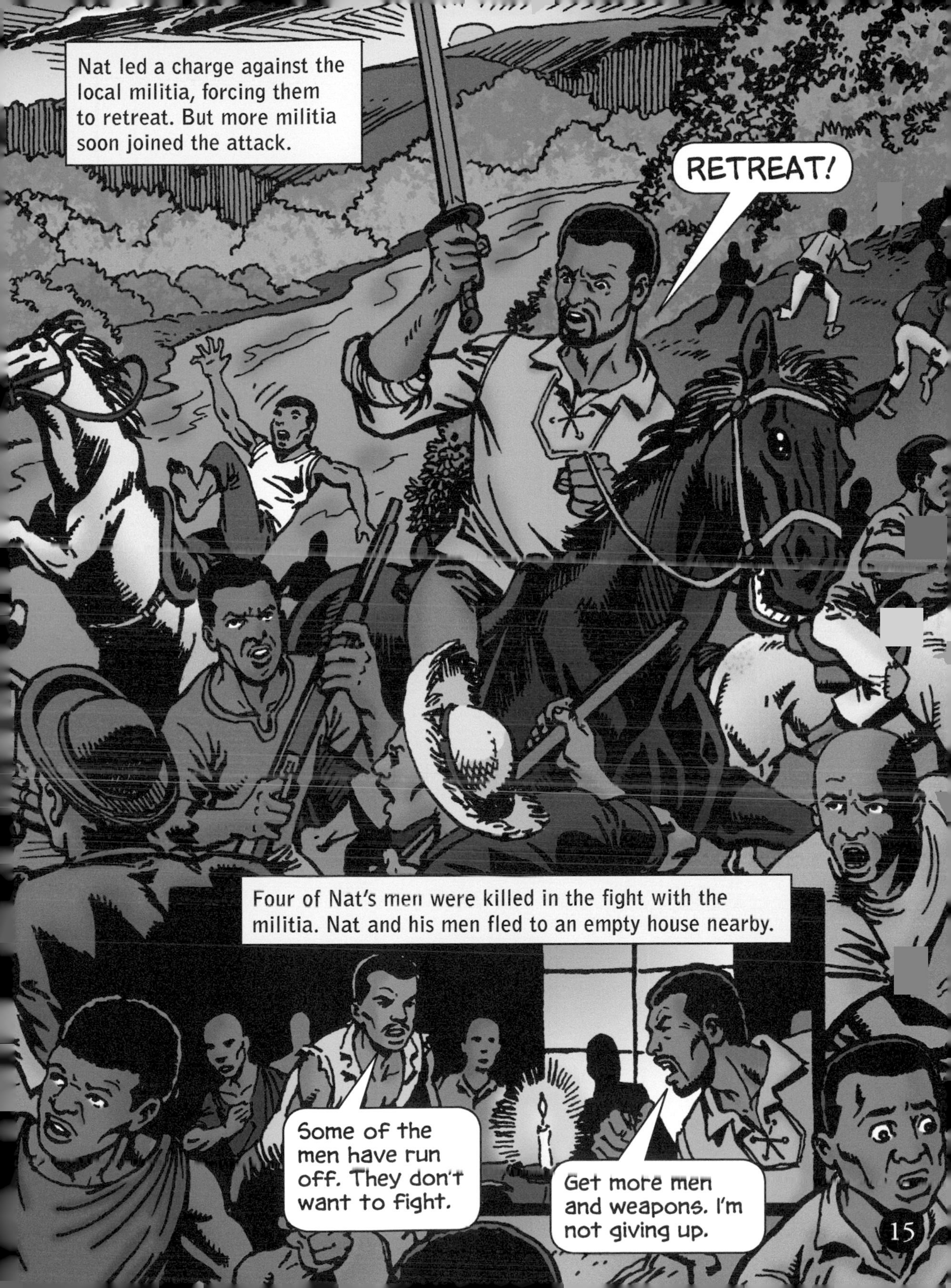
Nat led a charge against the local militia, forcing them to retreat. But more militia soon joined the attack.
RETREAT!
Four of Nat's men were killed in the fight with the militia. Nat and his men fled to an empty house nearby.
Some of the men have run off. They don't want to fight.
Get more men and weapons. I'm not giving up.

Chapter 3
CRUSHING A REBELLION

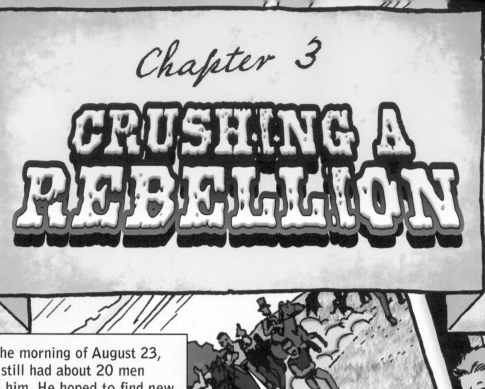

On the morning of August 23, Nat still had about 20 men with him. He hoped to find new recruits at the home of Samuel Blunt. Nat wanted to make sure the family was gone.

Samuel, his son Simon, and several other men were hiding in the home.

Go ahead and fire, Hark. See if anyone is there.

Get your guns ready, boys.

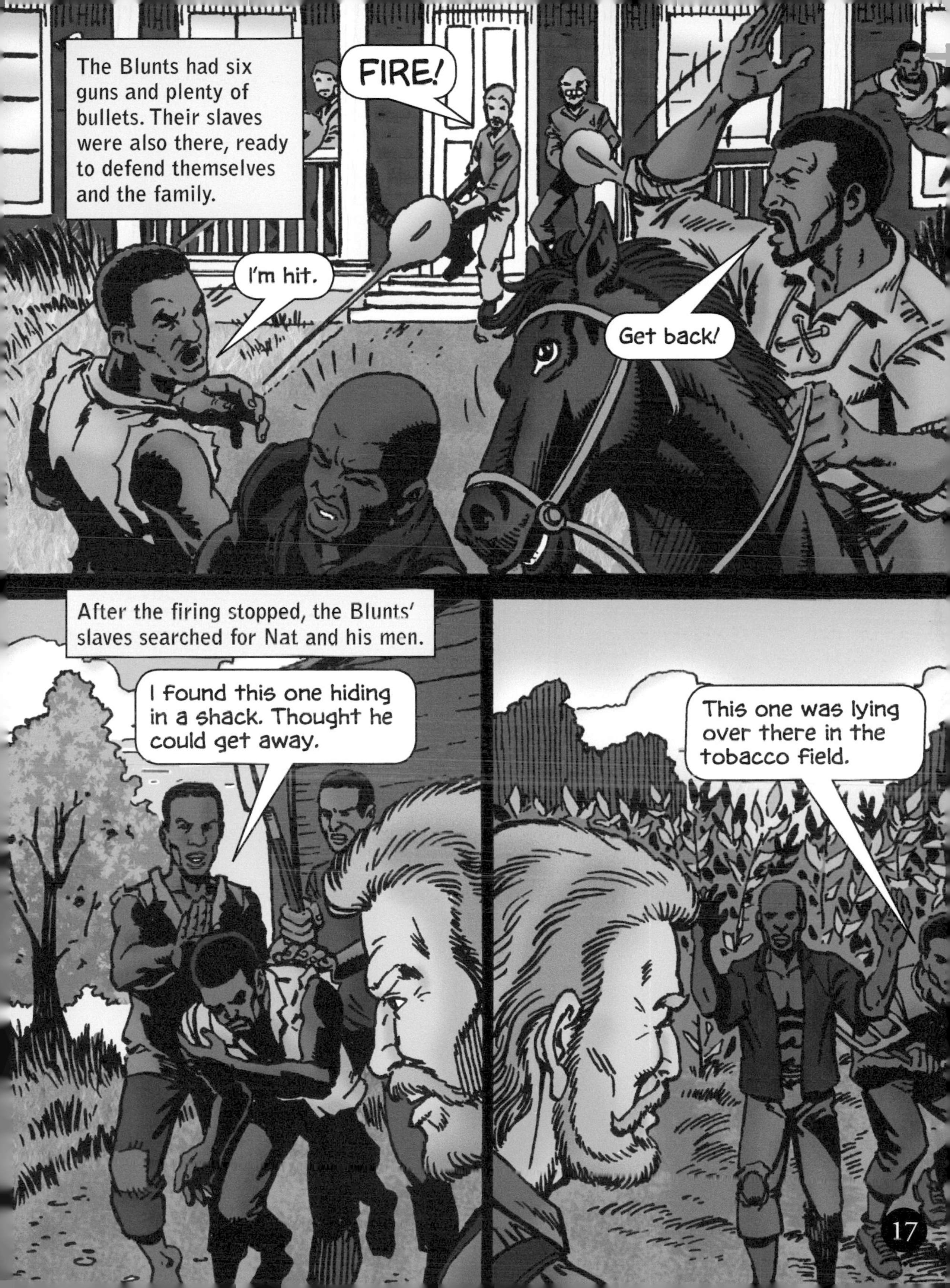
The Blunts had six guns and plenty of bullets. Their slaves were also there, ready to defend themselves and the family.
FIRE!
I'm hit.
Get back!
After the firing stopped, the Blunts' slaves searched for Nat and his men.
I found this one hiding in a shack. Thought he could get away.
This one was lying over there in the tobacco field.

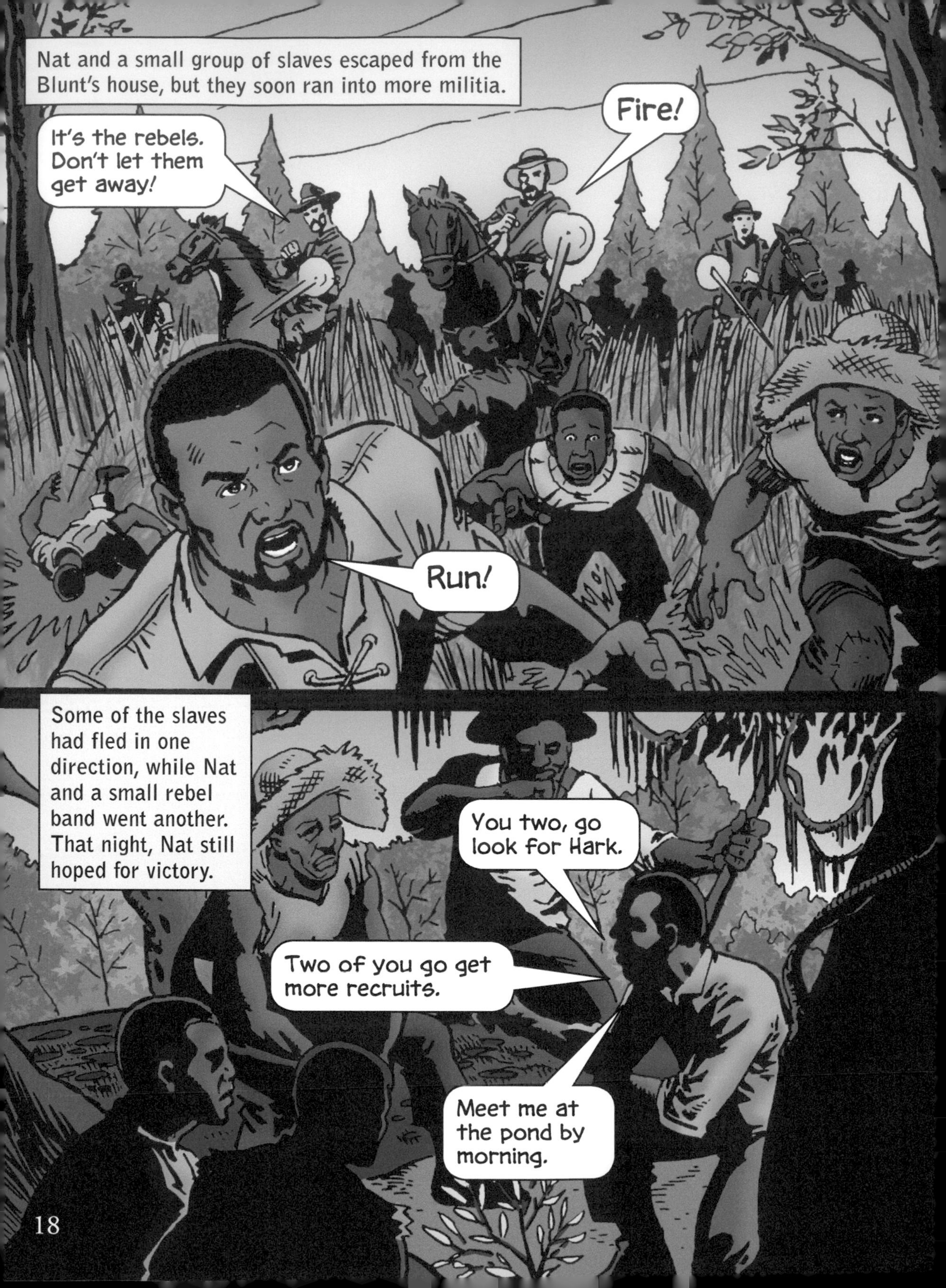
Nat and a small group of slaves escaped from the Blunt's house, but they soon ran into more militia.
It's the rebels. Don't let them get away!
Fire!
Run!
Some of the slaves had fled in one direction, while Nat and a small rebel band went another. That night, Nat still hoped for victory.
You two, go look for Hark.
Two of you go get more recruits.
Meet me at the pond by morning.

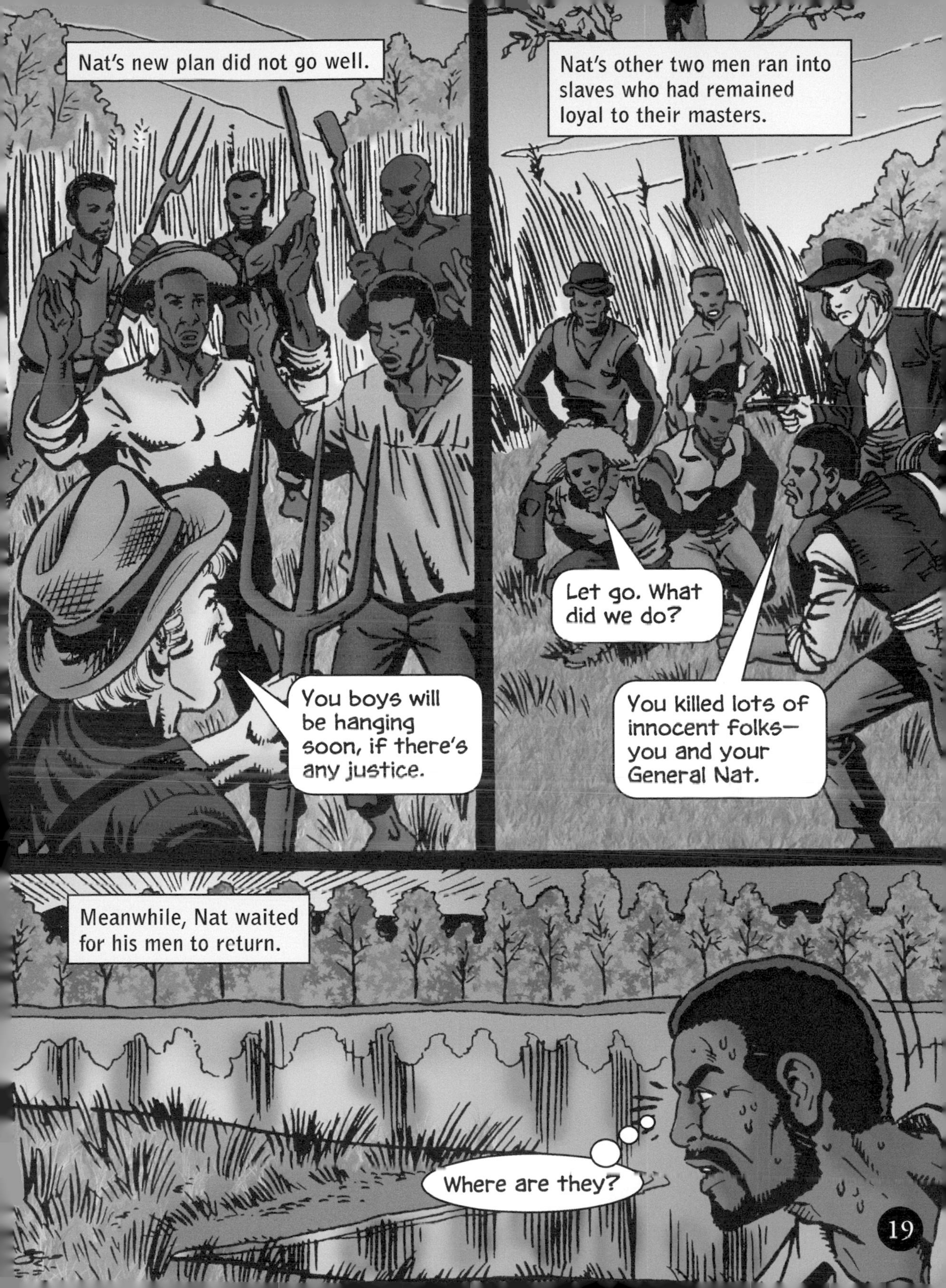
Nat's new plan did not go well.
You boys will be hanging soon, if there's any justice.
Nat's other two men ran into slaves who had remained loyal to their masters.
Let go. What did we do?
You killed lots of innocent folks— you and your General Nat.
Meanwhile, Nat waited for his men to return.
Where are they?

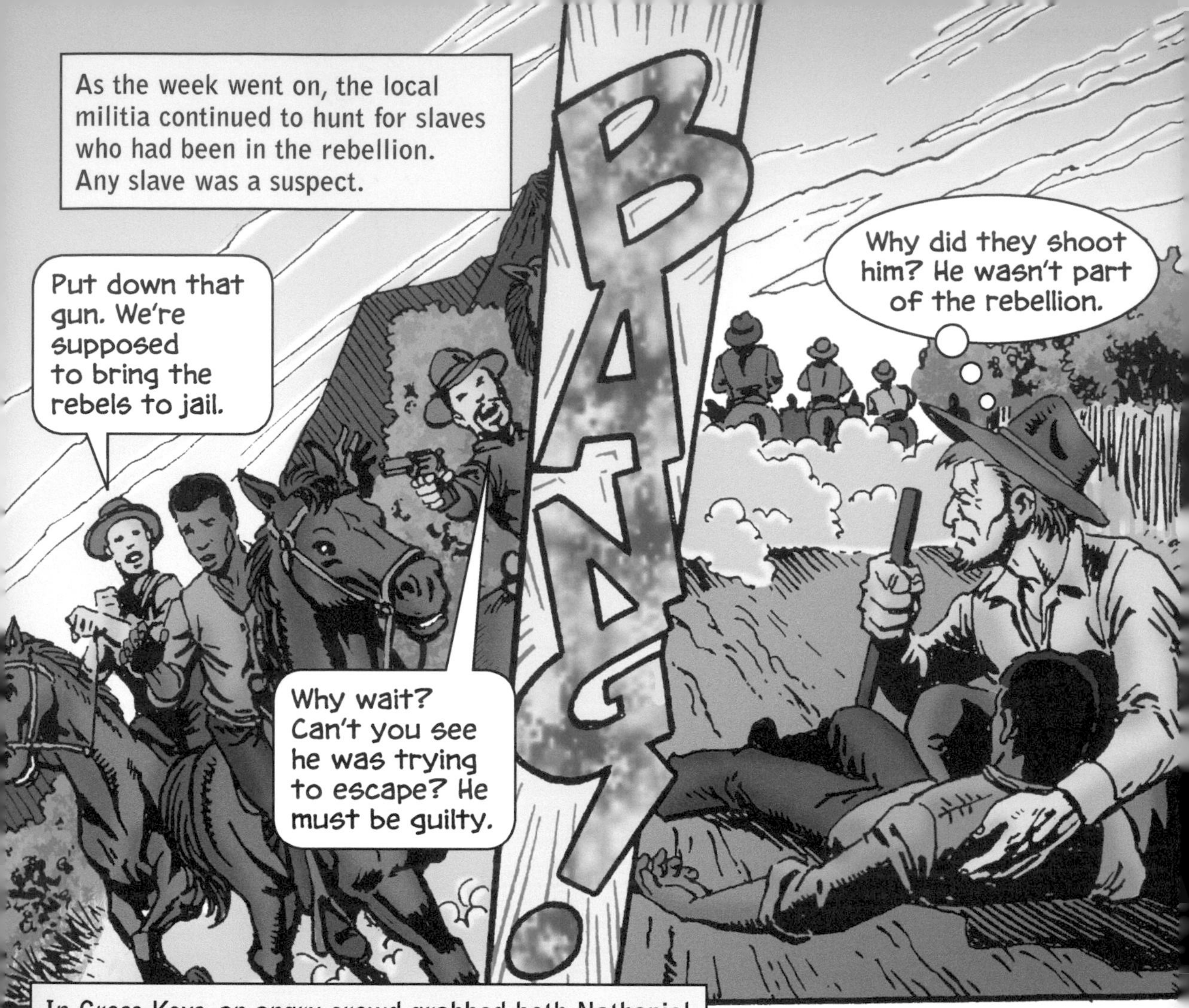
As the week went on, the local militia continued to hunt for slaves who had been in the rebellion. Any slave was a suspect.
Put down that gun. We're supposed to bring the rebels to jail.
Why wait? Can't you see he was trying to escape? He must be guilty.
BANG!
Why did they shoot him? He wasn't part of the rebellion.

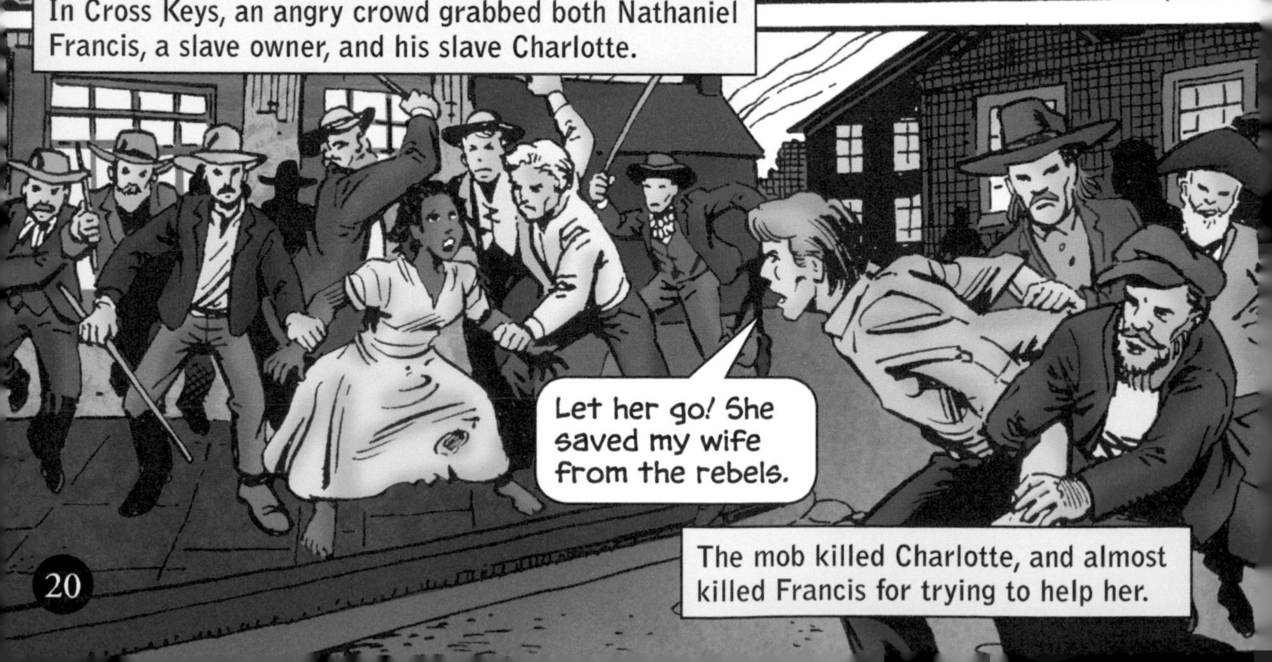
In Cross Keys, an angry crowd grabbed both Nathaniel Francis, a slave owner, and his slave Charlotte.
Let her go! She saved my wife from the rebels.
The mob killed Charlotte, and almost killed Francis for trying to help her.

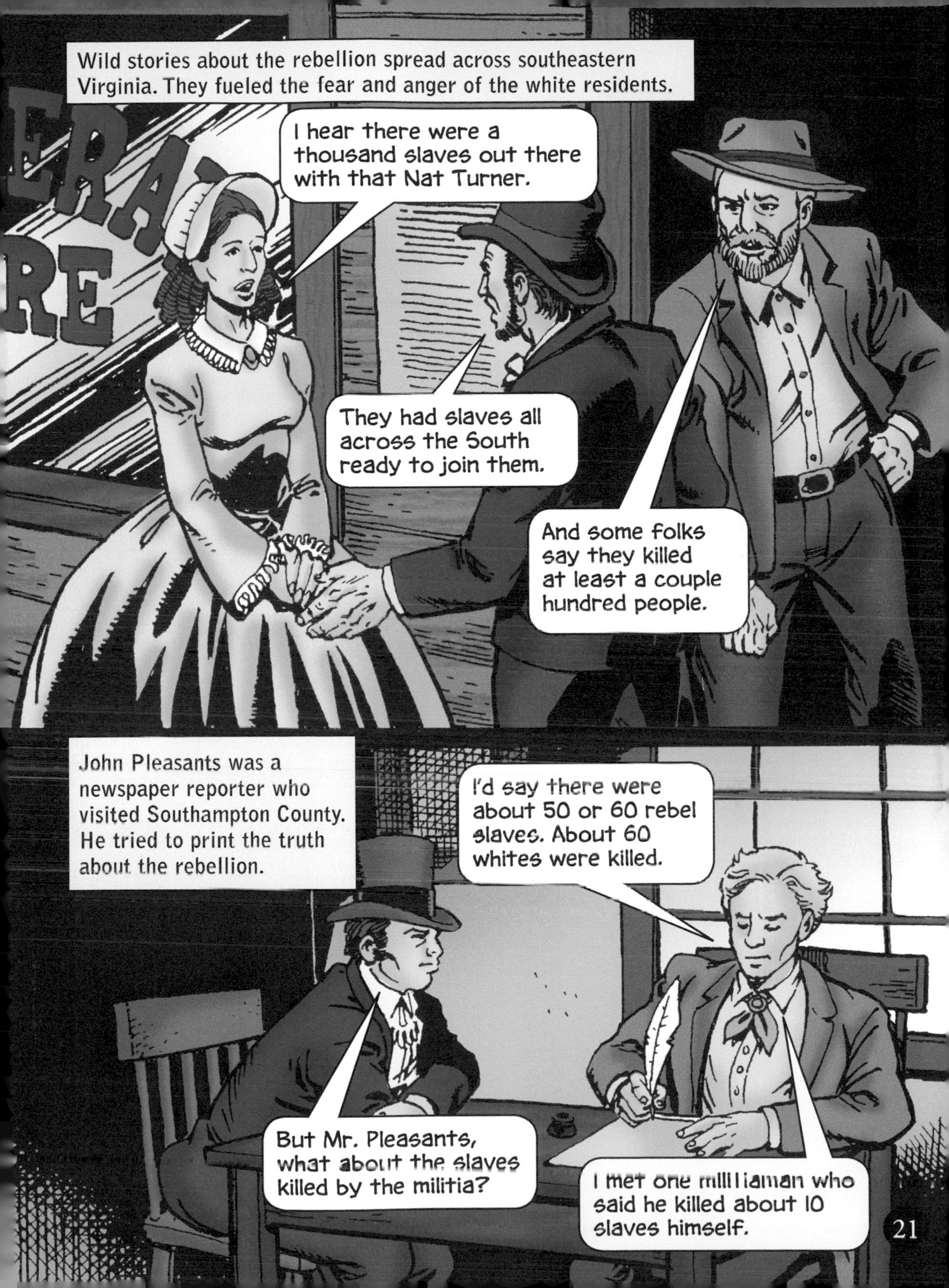

Wild stories about the rebellion spread across southeastern Virginia. They fueled the fear and anger of the white residents.
I hear there were a thousand slaves out there with that Nat Turner.
They had slaves all across the South ready to join them.
And some folks say they killed at least a couple hundred people.
John Pleasants was a newspaper reporter who visited Southampton County. He tried to print the truth about the rebellion.
I'd say there were about 50 or 60 rebel slaves. About 60 whites were killed.
But Mr. Pleasants, what about the slaves killed by the militia?
I met one militiaman who said he killed about 10 slaves himself.

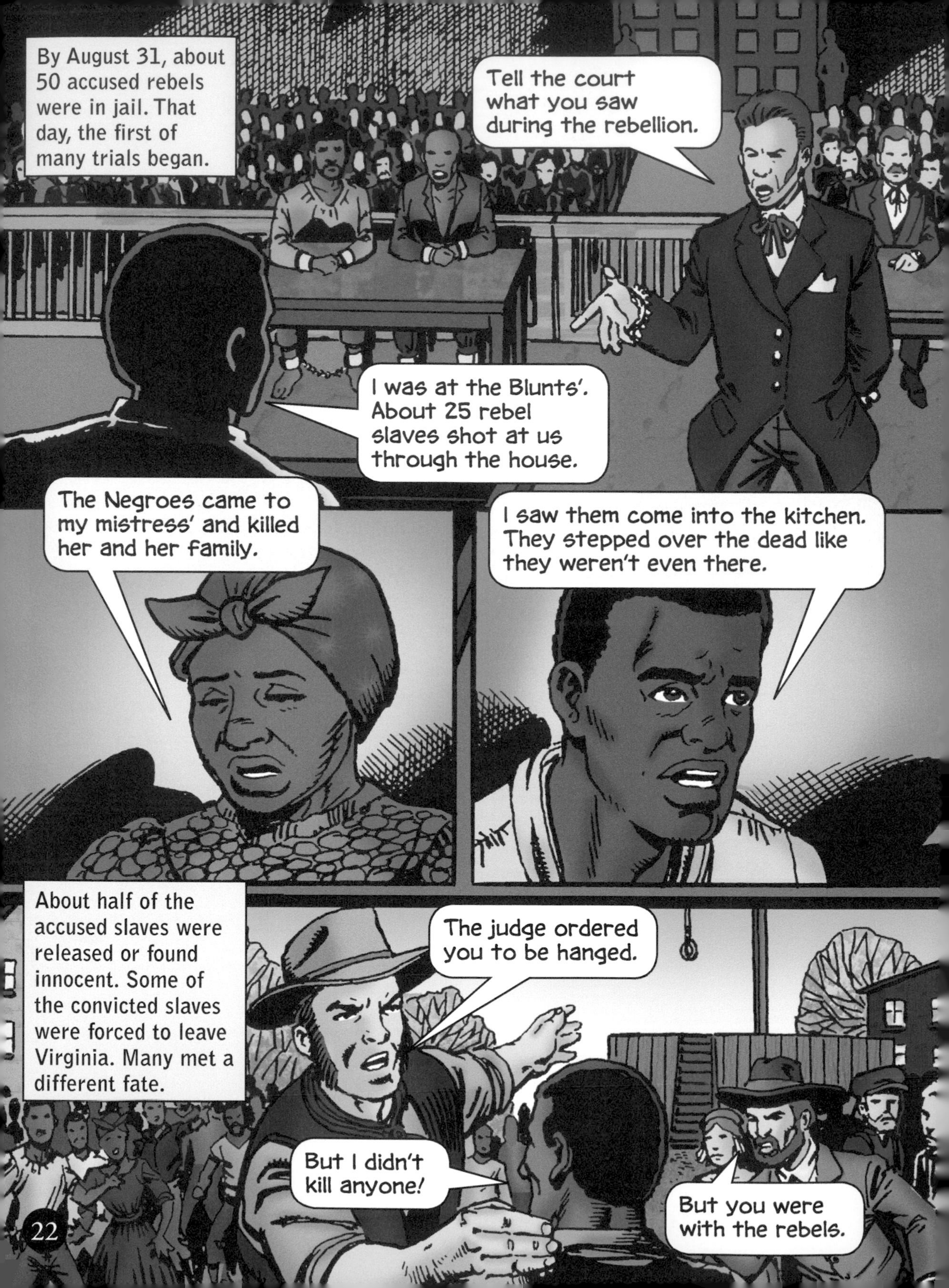
By August 31, about 50 accused rebels were in jail. That day, the first of many trials began.
Tell the court what you saw during the rebellion.
I was at the Blunts'. About 25 rebel slaves shot at us through the house.
The Negroes came to my mistress' and killed her and her family.
I saw them come into the kitchen. They stepped over the dead like they weren't even there.
About half of the accused slaves were released or found innocent. Some of the convicted slaves were forced to leave Virginia. Many met a different fate.
The judge ordered you to be hanged.
But I didn't kill anyone!
But you were with the rebels.

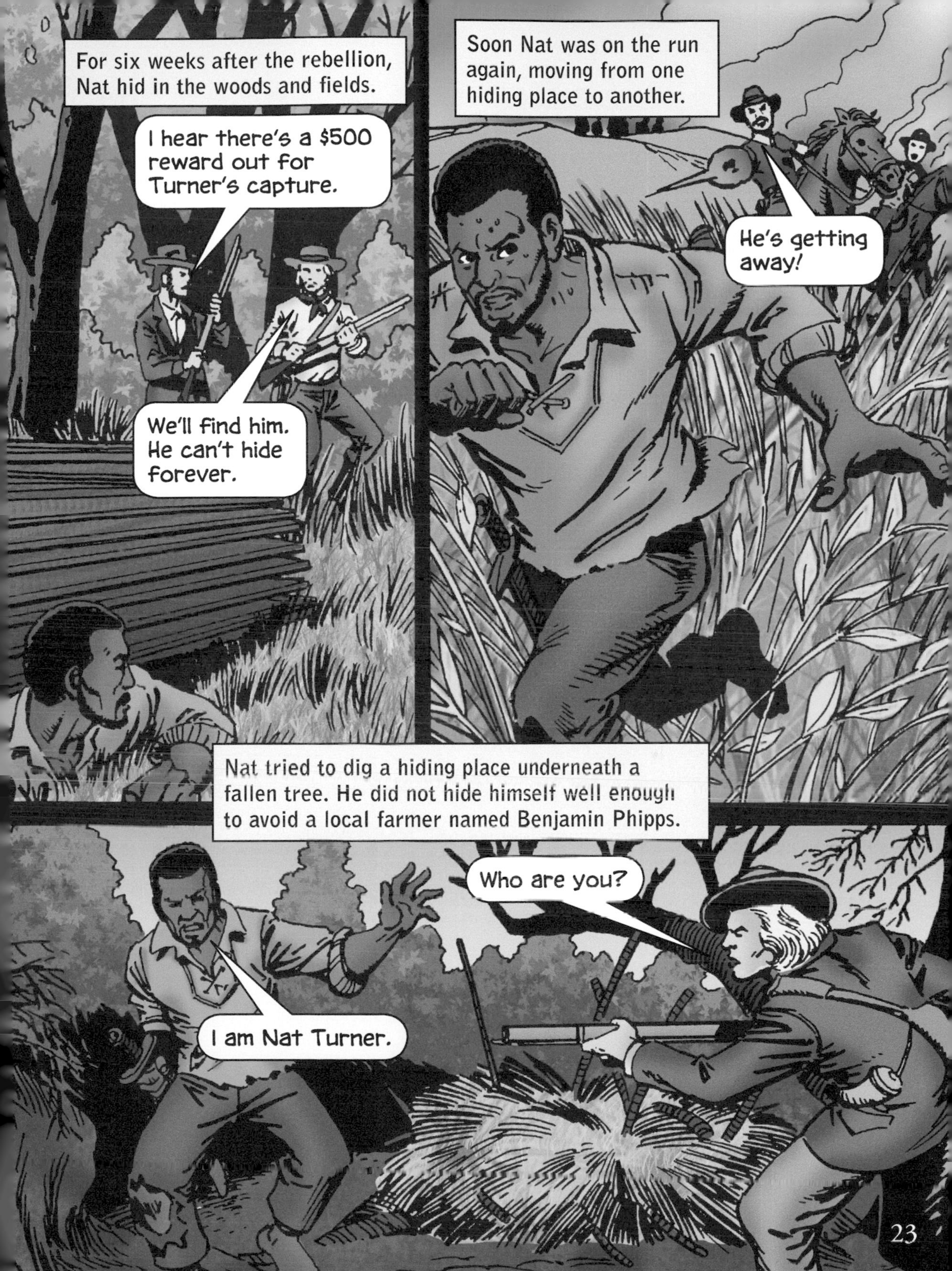

For six weeks after the rebellion, Nat hid in the woods and fields.
I hear there's a $500 reward out for Turner's capture.
We'll find him. He can't hide forever.
Soon Nat was on the run again, moving from one hiding place to another.
He's getting away!
Nat tried to dig a hiding place underneath a fallen tree. He did not hide himself well enough to avoid a local farmer named Benjamin Phipps.
Who are you?
I am Nat Turner.

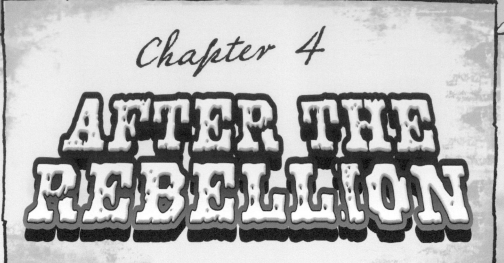

Chapter 4
AFTER THE REBELLION

On October 30, Phipps brought Nat to local officials, who marched him to jail.

That monster! We should kill him now, for what he did.

He'll get his day in court.

We still have a lot to learn about "General Nat."

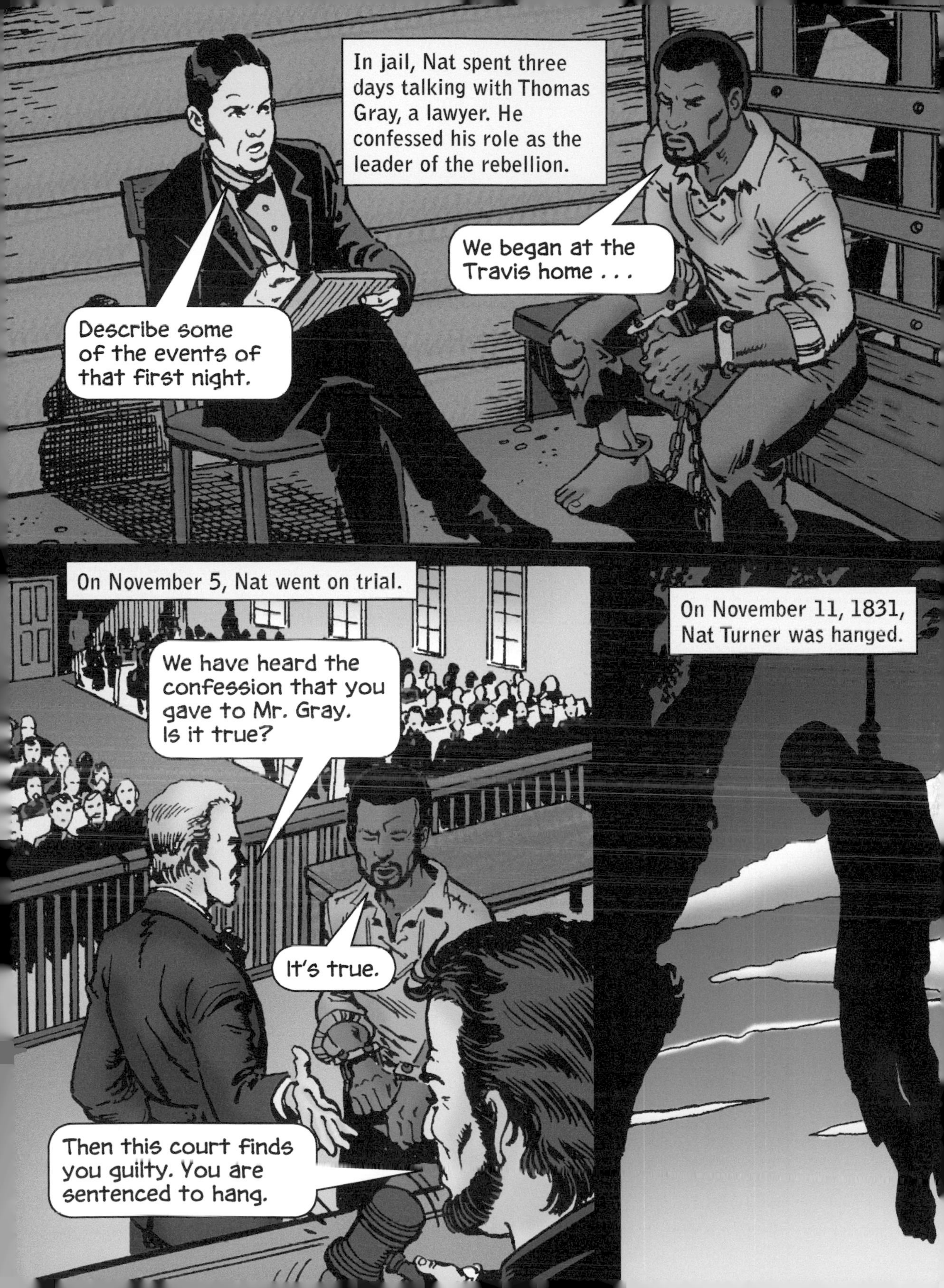
In jail, Nat spent three days talking with Thomas Gray, a lawyer. He confessed his role as the leader of the rebellion.
Describe some of the events of that first night.
We began at the Travis home . . .
On November 5, Nat went on trial.
We have heard the confession that you gave to Mr. Gray. Is it true?
It's true.
Then this court finds you guilty. You are sentenced to hang.
On November 11, 1831, Nat Turner was hanged.

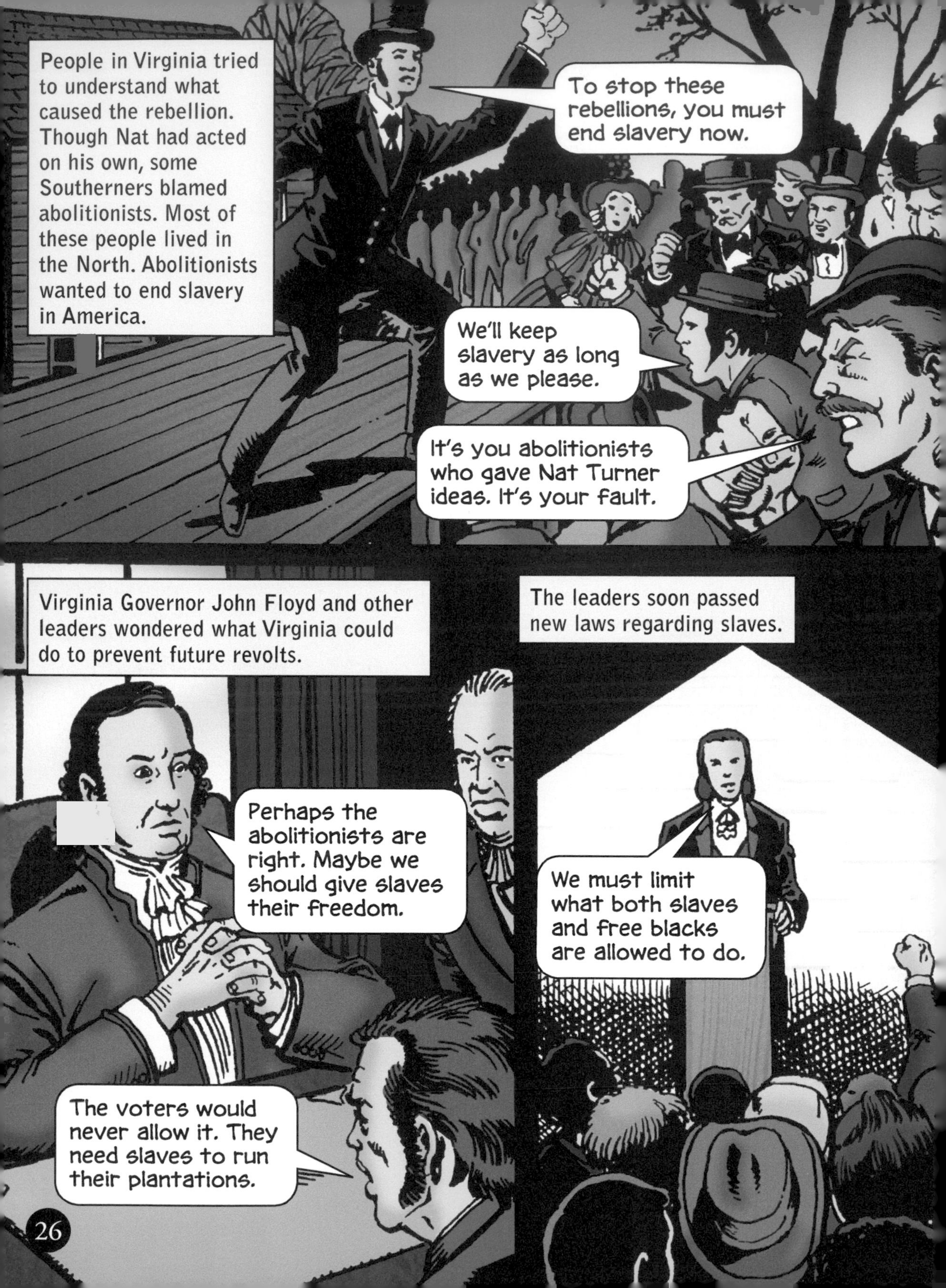
People in Virginia tried to understand what caused the rebellion. Though Nat had acted on his own, some Southerners blamed abolitionists. Most of these people lived in the North. Abolitionists wanted to end slavery in America.
To stop these rebellions, you must end slavery now.
We'll keep slavery as long as we please.
It's you abolitionists who gave Nat Turner ideas. It's your fault.
Virginia Governor John Floyd and other leaders wondered what Virginia could do to prevent future revolts.
Perhaps the abolitionists are right. Maybe we should give slaves their freedom.
The voters would never allow it. They need slaves to run their plantations.
The leaders soon passed new laws regarding slaves.
We must limit what both slaves and free blacks are allowed to do.

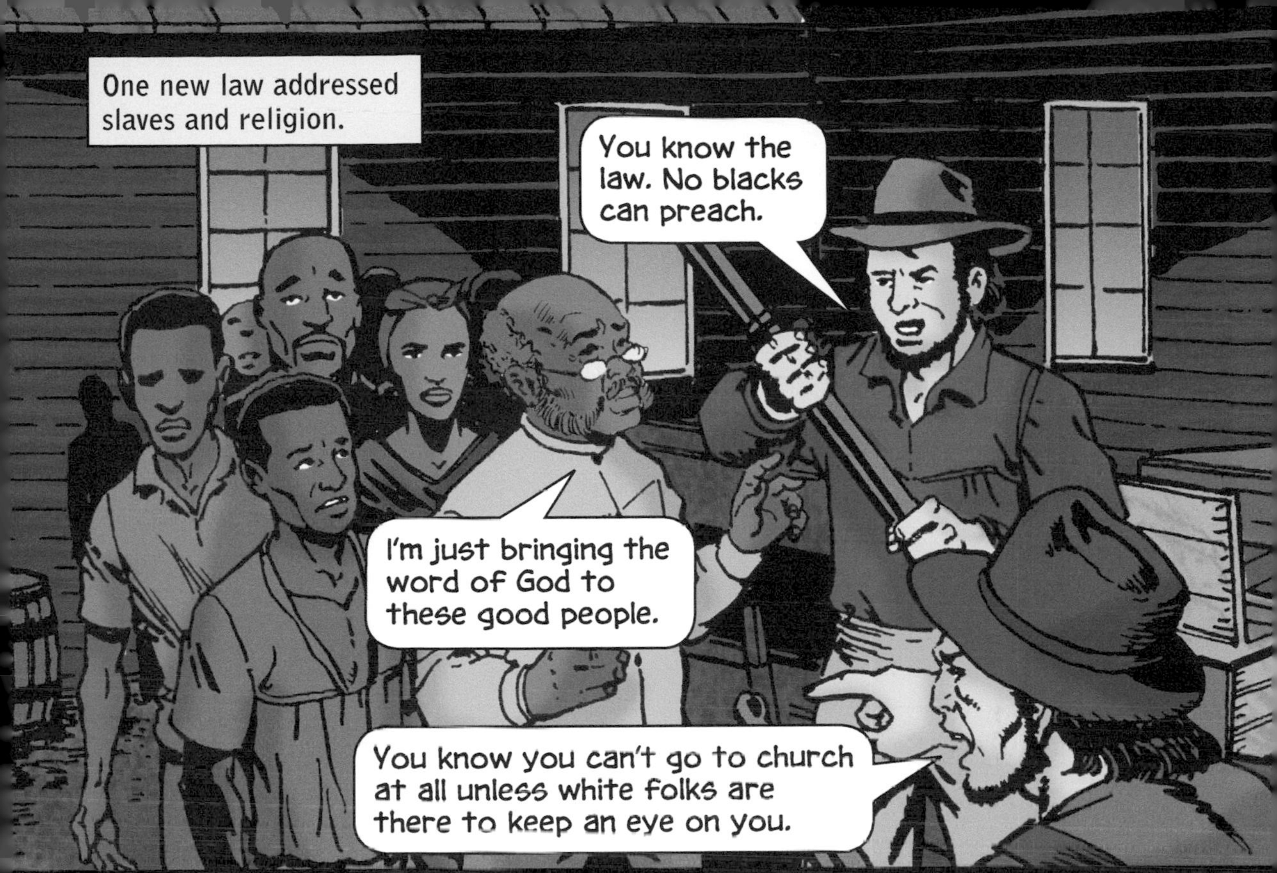
One new law addressed slaves and religion.
You know the law. No blacks can preach.
I'm just bringing the word of God to these good people.
You know you can't go to church at all unless white folks are there to keep an eye on you.

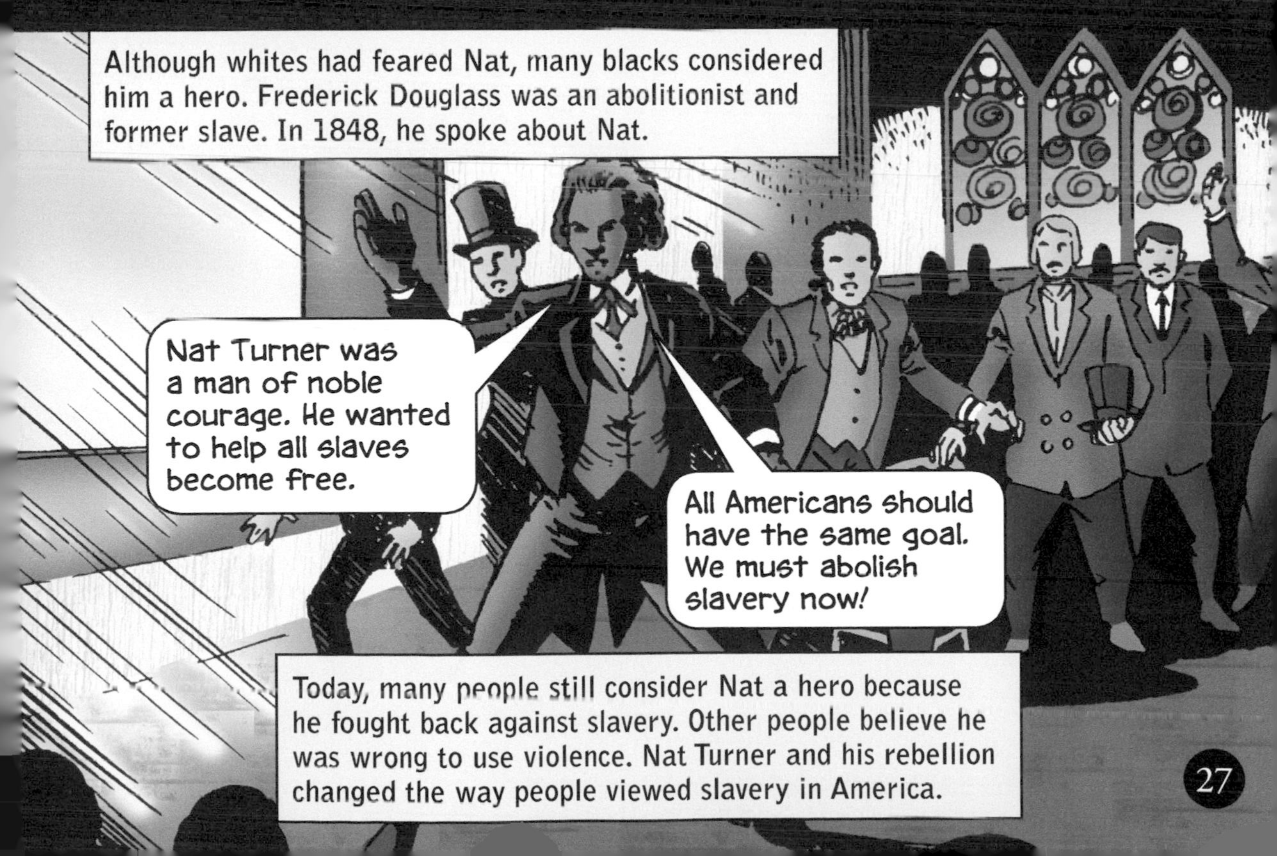
Although whites had feared Nat, many blacks considered him a hero. Frederick Douglass was an abolitionist and former slave. In 1848, he spoke about Nat.
Nat Turner was a man of noble courage. He wanted to help all slaves become free.
All Americans should have the same goal. We must abolish slavery now!
Today, many people still consider Nat a hero because he fought back against slavery. Other people believe he was wrong to use violence. Nat Turner and his rebellion changed the way people viewed slavery in America.

NAT TURNER'S SLAVE REBELLION

Nat Turner was born October 2, 1800. After Nat's birth, his mother, Nancy, considered killing her son to spare him a life of slavery.

At the start of Nat's rebellion, Southampton County had a population of just over 16,000. Almost half of these people were slaves.

Many slaves protected their owners during the rebellion. At one house, a slave stuffed a cloth in the mouth of a crying child so the rebel slaves would not know where the family was hiding.

Some people feared that Nat's rebellion would spread into North Carolina. The people of that state did not have proof that their slaves would rebel. Still, some people killed innocent slaves.

Officials in Norfolk, Virginia, asked the U.S. military to help fight Nat and his men. Marines and sailors were sent to Southampton County, but the rebellion had ended by the time they arrived.

The $500 reward offered for capturing Nat would be equal to just over $10,000 today.

During the trials, a slave girl named Beck said that she had heard some slaves talking about killing their masters months before Nat's rebellion. Several slaves who lived outside of Southampton County were convicted because of what Beck said. The men said they were innocent, and many people doubted Beck's claims.

Thomas Gray published *The Confessions of Nat Turner* soon after Nat was hanged. Printed and sold as a pamphlet, Gray's *The Confessions of Nat Turner* gives a detailed account of the rebellion. Historians, however, doubt the accuracy of Gray's account. They believe Gray used his own words, not Nat's, to tell about the rebellion.

GLOSSARY

abolitionist (ab-uh-LISH-uh-nist)—a person who worked to end slavery before the Civil War

eclipse (e-KLIPS)—when the moon comes between the sun and the earth so that all or part of the sun's light is blocked out

militia (muh-LISH-uh)—a group of civilians who form an army during emergencies

preach (PREECH)—to give a religious talk to people, especially during a church service

prophet (PROF-it)—someone who claims to speak for God

vision (VIZH-uhn)—a dream that conveys a message

INTERNET SITES

FactHound offers a safe, fun way to find Internet sites related to this book. All of the sites on FactHound have been researched by our staff.

Here's how:

1. Visit *www.facthound.com*
2. Type in this special code **0736854908** for age-appropriate sites. Or enter a search word related to this book for a more general search.
3. Click on the **Fetch It** button.

FactHound will fetch the best sites for you!

READ MORE

Bisson, Terry. *Nat Turner: Slave Revolt Leader.*
Black Americans of Achievement. Philadelphia: Chelsea
House, 2005.

De Capua, Sarah. *Abolitionists: A Force for Change.* Journey
to Freedom. Chanhassen, Minn.: Child's World, 2003.

Gregson, Susan R. *Nat Turner: Rebellious Slave.* Let
Freedom Ring. Mankato, Minn.: Capstone Press 2003.

Isaacs, Sally Senzell. *Life on a Southern Plantation.* Picture
the Past. Chicago: Heinemann, 2001.

BIBLIOGRAPHY

Documenting the American South. *The Confessions of Nat
Turner.* (http://docsouth.unc.edu/turner/turner.html).

Greenberg, Kenneth S. *Nat Turner: A Slave Rebellion in
History and Memory.* New York: Oxford University
Press, 2003.

Oates, Stephen B. *The Fires of Jubilee: Nat Turner's Fierce
Rebellion.* New York: Harper & Row, 1975.

Tragle, Henry Irving. *The Southampton Slave Revolt of
1831.* New York: Vintage Books, 1973.

INDEX